Poems From The Heart

Zaytoona Nur

Poems from The Heart

Copyright © *Zaytoona Nur,* 2025
All Rights Reserved

This book is subject to the condition that no part of this book is to be reproduced, transmitted in any form or means; electronic or mechanical, stored in a retrieval system, photocopied, recorded, scanned, or otherwise. Any of these actions require the proper written permission of the author.

Table of Contents

Introduction From the Author 1
Chapter 1: Modesty and Identity 3
    The Muslim Woman 3
    When You Look At Me 4
    The Simple Garment 5
Chapter 2 Spirituality and Connection 6
    The Religion of Islam 6
    Imaan 8
    Wake Up Oh Believers 10
    Ya Allah 12
    The Call from the Creator 14
    The Connection 15
    Intention 16
Chapter 3 Gratitude and Reflection 17
    Thank You, Oh Allah! 17
    Who Am I? 19
    Thoughts of a Muslim 21
    Characteristics of a Muslim 23
    Time 24
Chapter 4 Islamic Practices and Celebrations 25
    Eidul-Fitr 25
    The Secret Tool 27
    My Salat 29
Chapter 5 Inspirational Figures in Islam 30
    Assallatu Wasallamu Allaika Ya Habibullah 30
    Aishah, One of the Wives of the Prophet (SAW) 31

Introduction
From the Author

I greet you with the beautiful greeting of Islam, Assalamu Alaykum (Peace be upon you), and thank you for your interest in this short book of poems from the heart. It is my intention to share my thoughts and feelings around different topics to highlight the beauty of my faith, Islam. As they say, sharing is caring! I have deliberately kept the poems short, sweet, and to the point to whet your appetite to seek knowledge. I really do hope you enjoy reading them with an open mind and heart. I enjoyed writing them for you.

Keep smiling. Blessed and be blessed,

Zaytoona Nur, 2025

Here is a little gem from my beautiful mother to get you thinking.

The Rocking Boat

From far I can see the waves,

Coming closer and bigger,

The boat is rocking, rocking till it rests on an island.

The island is beautiful and peaceful

Only a short stay but we must move on.

[In this version, the "waves" and "island" are metaphors for life's journey and a place of spiritual peace. The "boat" represents the individual's heart or soul navigating life's challenges until it finds rest in a state of inner peace and connection to faith. The idea of a "short stay" on an "island" can be interpreted as the transient nature of earthly life in Islamic teachings, with a focus on the eternal afterlife].

Chapter 1: Modesty and Identity

The Muslim Woman

See how she walks swiftly and gently,

With her modesty shining through.

See how her eyes never rise,

Even at the sight of temptation.

See how her confidence carries her through,

The sniggering groups of people.

See how strong-willed she is,

With no fear whatsoever.

See how respected she is,

With her outstanding character. Have you ever stopped to think,

Why she is like this?

Have you ever thought,

What drives her to be different amongst other women?

Have you ever thought,

What makes her so special to the people of understanding?

She is a pious Muslim Woman,

Who far exceeds the value of the treasures of this world.

When You Look At Me

When you look at me,

What do you see?

Someone restricted within her beliefs?

Cannot think or gain freedom like everyone else?

When you look at me,

What do you see?

Someone illiterate, backward, and boring?

Well, I beg to differ.

This is not me.

The true me holds my belief with dignity,

The true me respects myself,

Enough not to expose it to the pleasures of the world.

You see, I know my worth is much more than worldly temptations.

The true me doesn't have to boast

About the knowledge I hold in order to use it.

To the world, I may be boring and backwards,

But to me, I am fulfilling my Islamic duties.

The Simple Garment

I am a Muslim,

A proud Muslim,

A lady with strong beliefs,

Why should I hide that fact?

The comments, the looks, the sniggering,

Don't care what people think,

I will still hold my head high,

I will still walk with bliss and dignity.

So simple is the garment,

Yet so effective at its job,

Protecting me from the eyes of the world,

Reminding me of Allah.

Stop… look… and think,

Do you truly want to be amongst the ignorant?

Do you truly want the lustful world?

Is it really worth sacrificing your Imaan?

Chapter 2
Spirituality and Connection

The Religion of Islam

Islam is a way of life, divinely chosen by Allah,

A path of peace and truth, in which no soul is left ajar.

It means complete submission to the One and Only Lord,

To Allah (SWT), whose guidance we cannot afford to ignore.

It teaches peace and justice, in harmony it stands,

Not something part-time, to shape with shifting sands.

We do not pick and choose, nor bend it to our will—

For Islam is a trust, a light, a truth, a seal.

So simple is this faith, in nature it aligns,

With every law and rhythm the world around us finds.

Through the noble Prophet (SAW), this guidance came to be,

In the Qur'an and his Sunnah, our path is clear to see.

Footnote:
A follower of Islam is called a **Muslim**.

The divine book in Islam is the **Qur'an**, revealed to the Prophet Muhammad (SAW) through divine revelation.

The way of the Prophet is known as the **Sunnah**, and his sayings are referred to as **Hadith**.

Imaan

Imaan is a beautiful gift, placed gently in the hearts of Believers,

A quiet light that brings peace, even in life's most difficult seasons.

It is a treasure, more precious than gold,

A jewel that shines within the soul.

It is believing in Allah, the Most High,

Trusting in His presence, though He is beyond the eye.

It is believing in His Angels, and yes, in the Jinn,

In the unseen world that surrounds us within.

It is believing in His divine books—sent as guides,

And in His noble Messengers who brought truth to our lives.

It is believing in the Last Day, the life after this one,

When all shall be gathered and justice shall be done.

It is knowing, deep down, that all things come from Him—

The good, the bad, the joy, the trials within.

But, dear Believers, please remember this,

Our Imaan is not fixed, it can waver or lift.

It rises with worship, with kindness, with prayer,

It weakens when we forget, or fall into despair.

So let us protect it, let us help it grow—

Step by step, day by day, steady and slow.

Footnote:

Understanding Imaan helps us take care of it.

It is not just something we have—it is something we must nurture.

May we all find ways to strengthen our Imaan each day, insha'Allah.

O Allah, help us to increase our Imaan — Ameen.

Wake Up Oh Believers

Wake up… wake up oh Believers, Wake up before it's too late.

Do you not see what is happening?

Do you not feel your hearts cry?

This world is a test, oh Believers.

Do not lose your way in it.

Do not sell your soul for it.

It will not last forever.

Allah is the Merciful,

Allah is the Oft-Forgiver.

So repent while you can, oh Believers.

Repent before it's too late.

Why do you fight amongst yourselves?

Fight yourselves instead.

Wake up your inner soul to the cry of your hearts.

Wake up before it's too late.

Listen to your inner soul.

Listen to your heart.

What is it crying out for?

What is it aching for?

Surrender to Allah, the Almighty, oh Believers.

Surrender to the true Friend.

The Friend that will be there for you in both the worlds.

The Friend that will fill your hearts with eternal Noor.

Wake up… wake up, oh Believers. Wake up before it's too late.

Ya Allah

Ya Allah… my heart is yearning,

Yearning for love,

Love that you bestow.

I feel so lonely, Lonely, lost, and confused.

Do I truly feel this way?

Or is it my imagination?

This ache in my heart

Oh Allah! It is making me weep.

It is you, oh Allah, that I turn to.

It is you, oh Allah, I yearn for.

Yearn for your love, mercy, and friendship.

Lonely and empty I may feel, but yet a Light is growing in my Heart.

And my heart fills with hope and contentment.

And it is then that I know,

Indeed I am not alone, oh Allah,

As I know you are with me.

Oh Allah, take me away from this materialistic life, And put me in a safe place where I will find tranquillity,

Serenity, and sustenance.

Take me away from the dark,

And put me in a fortress of your Noor and protection.

This world is nothing to me… oh Allah.

A mere Jannah for the non-believers.

Oh Allah, why am I craving, aching for you?

Is it because my time has come to be near to you?

Or is it because you are smiling upon me?

Oh Allah, my heart is yearning,

Yearning for your love.

The Call from the Creator

I am here,

Can you see me? I am right here beside you,

Can you feel me?

I am close by,

Can you sense me?

I am calling,

Can you hear me?

This is my call for you my servant,

So call upon me and I shall answer you.

The Connection

O Allah, what is this pull I feel, so deep within my heart?

This ache, this yearning to belong, tearing me gently apart.

Why do these tears fall quietly, as if I already know—

The place my soul remembers, the place I long to go?

And deep within, I hear it rise,

The ancient words that lift the skies:

Labaik Allahumma Labaik,

Labaik laa shareeka laka labaik,

Innal hamda wan-ni'mata laka wal mulk,

Laa shareeka lak.

This is the call of the soul, the echo of every heart,

The sacred longing carried in us, from the very start.

Feel the **taqwa** running through the blood, with every step of **Tawaaf**,

Feel His presence wrap around you, guiding you to cleanse your path.

With each breath, purify your soul, let your burdens fall away,

And soak in the blessed moments that your heart will never betray.

Absorb the air, the light, the peace—let it settle deep within,

For this is the journey of a lifetime, where every soul begins again.

Intention

O Believers, do you know how important it is—

To carry the right intention in all that you do?

The smallest action, when done for His sake,

Can bring you Allah's blessings, His mercy, His love too.

Once in a while, pause and ask yourself:

Have I truly got the right intention?

Am I doing this for Allah, with sincerity in my heart?

Or has my purpose slipped into another direction?

A pure intention is a light that guides,

It brings ease in this world, and reward in the next.

It turns daily deeds into acts of worship,

And gently steers the soul to what is best.

O Believers, do not overlook this truth—

That every act holds meaning, every step is seen,

So long as your heart is firm in faith,

And your intention is clean.

O Allah, help us to purify what lies within,

To do it all for You, and You alone—Ameen.

Chapter 3
Gratitude and Reflection

Thank You, Oh Allah!

Thank You, oh Allah, for this life You have given,

For letting me walk upon Your earth, under Your sky.

But why does sadness fill my heart at times—

When I forget to truly cherish this gift from on high?

Thank You, oh Allah, for my eyes that see Your beauty,

The colours of Your creation, the wonders You unfold.

But why do I not use them to read Your divine words,

The Qur'an—so perfect, so timeless, so bold?

Thank You, oh Allah, for the voice You gave me,

A means to speak, to comfort, to pray.

But why do I not call upon You more,

Why do I let my words waste away?

Thank You, oh Allah, for the gift of hearing,

For the chance to hear the Adhan echo clear.

But why do I not hear my own soul weeping,

Yearning for You, with taqwa and fear?

Thank You, oh Allah, for the strength in my hands,

Hands that can build, hands that can serve.

But why do I not raise them high—

To hold Islam's banner with love and nerve?

Oh Allah, I beg for Your mercy, from deep within my soul,

You are the Oft-Forgiving, the One who makes us whole.

I am only human, weak in a world full of trials,

Struggling at times, yet walking Your path in miles.

Oh Allah, increase my Imaan and taqwa each day,

Let it shine so brightly that it awakens hearts astray.

Let me be a light, a reminder, a guide—

To draw others gently to Your mercy and pride.

Oh Allah, thank You for making me a Believer true,

A soul that longs for the Aakhirah and returns to You.

Who Am I?

I am a flower with no scent,

Yet I sway happily in the breeze.

Rooted firm within the pot—

Content with what Allah has decreed for me.

I followed the advice of my mentor,

And I am at peace with the path I chose.

No bitterness rests in my heart,

Only the quiet fear of Allah, the One who knows.

I place my trust in Him alone,

And leave behind the noise of this world.

Its glitter does not call to me—

For I have turned my gaze elsewhere, unfurled.

I long only for a spiritual love,

A connection deep, serene, and true.

I wait for the eternal home

That Allah has promised to the hearts that renew.

I do not expect the world to understand me,

Nor do I need its fleeting praise.

If Allah is pleased with who I am—

That is enough to light my days.

So, what does this tell you about me?

Thoughts of a Muslim

I look around and wonder...

What is the meaning behind all that I see?

What is the purpose of everything happening around me?

What is the reason for my very existence?

Subhanallah.

The moon, the sun, the stars — how perfectly they move in harmony.

I pause and reflect...

How can I deny a Creator?

Can there be creation without a Creator?

Can something come from nothing?

Surely, we are here for a reason.

Did the Prophet (SAW), and those before him, come without purpose?

Did the events in this beautiful faith occur without meaning?

Islam is like dipping into the ocean.

The more you learn, the more your heart longs to seek.

If you saw this world as a test for the next...

Would you not change how you live?

Would you not rethink your ways?

I am not a scholar or philosopher —

Just a simple Muslim.

And these are my thoughts.

Characteristics of a Muslim

A Muslim obeys parents and honours the old.

A Muslim is truthful, sincere, and bold.

A Muslim is kind, forgiving, and fair.

A Muslim avoids hurtful words or a glare.

A Muslim gives charity, lends a hand.

Cares for orphans, as Allah has planned.

Follows the Qur'an and Sunnah with grace,

Strives to walk in the Prophet's (SAW) trace.

A Muslim upholds the Pillars with pride —

Shahadah, Salat, and Zakat as guide,

Sawm in Ramadan, and Hajj if they can.

Seeking Allah's pleasure in every plan.

Time

Time is precious — we all know that.

It keeps moving forward, never looks back.

Every second brings us near,

To our Creator, crystal clear.

Time is a blessing from the Most High,

To be used well, before it flies by.

Those who live with purpose each day,

Are truly blessed in every way.

Dear believer, do not delay —

Your youth will not forever stay.

Spend your wealth before it's gone,

Use your strength while it is strong.

And most of all, take care, take heed —

Do not let this world feed your greed.

Use your time while it is in your hand,

To seek Allah and understand.

Chapter 4
Islamic Practices and Celebrations

Eidul-Fitr

Subhanallah! What a beautiful day,

The sun is out after hiding away.

Frost on the road like diamonds shine,

Snow wraps the trees in a soft white line.

It is cold, yet hearts feel light,

The spirit of Eid makes the world bright.

Ya Allah, what a scent in the air,

A day of joy, beyond compare.

After a month of striving and grace,

Allah has blessed us in this place.

Children beam with angelic smiles,

In new clothes, walking proud for miles.

Girls show off their hennaed hands,

Boys join Salat as the day expands.

At the mosque, warm hugs are shared,

Peace and harmony, beautifully paired.

See how they glow from deep within,

A joy that only faith can bring.

Let this light reach every land,

A gift of Eid from Allah's hand.

Wishing you Eid that fills your heart,

With mercy and a brand new start.

May Allah bless your every day,

With love, with peace, in every way. Ameen.

The Secret Tool

Would you like to gain the pleasure of Allah

with a simple, modest act?

Would you like to practise what our Beloved Prophet (SAW)

did even in his final moments?

Have you stopped to consider

what could be so special

in helping you attain divine rewards?

What could be so effective

in keeping you steadfast

in the recitation of the Kalimah

on your deathbed?

What could be so powerful

that it cleanses your heart

and strengthens your obedience to Allah?

Allahu Akbar, oh Believers!

See how merciful Allah is—

He wants His servants to succeed

in this world and the next.

All you have to do

is brush your teeth with the humble Miswak!

Did you know it holds many physical benefits too?

From sharpening your memory,

creating Noor on your face,

strengthening your eyesight,

aiding digestion,

curing headaches,

to strengthening your gums and preventing tooth decay?

The Miswak is a secret tool for true believers.

So, use it as much as you can.

My Salat

When life's difficulties leave me tired…

When its challenges make me upset…

When calamities fall and I see no way out…

In my Salat, I find peace and calm.

In my Salat, I find answers and light,

A way through the trials of this dunya.

In my Salat, I find strength and help

From my Creator — the Almighty, the Wise.

Without Salat, I am lost and alone,

Drifting in this world without direction.

Oh Believers, do you see the power of Salat?

It keeps the heart tied to its Source.

Footnote:

Salat refers to the five daily prayers performed at set times throughout the day. It is a divine prescription from Allah for navigating this worldly life. A Muslim is truly recognised through their commitment to Salat — not just as a religious duty, but as a source of strength, peace, and grounding. It offers a moment to step away from the noise of the dunya and reconnect with the Creator. Salat is more than a ritual; it is a private, sacred conversation with Allah — a moment where the heart speaks and He listens.

Chapter 5
Inspirational Figures in Islam

Assallatu Wasallamu Allaika Ya Habibullah

Blessed is he, the Prophet of Allah,
Blessed is his whole being.

Blessed is he, an exemplary figure,
Blessed is his noble character.

Blessed is he, the Beloved of Allah,
Blessed is his smile and charm.

Blessed is he, the Seal of the Prophets,
Blessed is his status and honour.

Blessed is he, the Mercy to the Worlds,
Blessed is his perfect soul.

Blessed is he, Allah's perfect creation,
Blessed is his Divine Noor.

Aishah, One of the Wives of the Prophet (SAW)

Peace be upon you, Lady Aishah (RA),

The daughter of Abu Bakr Siddique (RA).

I honour and respect you, Oh Aishah,

For showing to the world

That a woman can be teachers of scholars and experts.

Your life is such an encouragement to us all,

As you have shown

That a woman can influence and inspire

Men and women alike.

Oh Aishah (RA), your words are studied

In faculties of literature,

And your legal sayings are studied

In colleges of law.

Yet, you have shown that a woman can also

Fulfil her duties

As a wife and a daughter.

Oh Allah, please help us all

To learn from this great lady – Ameen.

www.ingramcontent.com/pod-product-compliance
Lightning Source LLC
Chambersburg PA
CBHW060413080526
44583CB00012B/558